Folk Music Greatest Hits

THE ABSOLUTE BIGGEST HITS OF MODERN FOLK MUSIC!
COMPLETE ORIGINAL SHEET MUSIC EDITIONS
INCLUDES MANY RARE PHOTOS

Catalog #07-1035

ISBN# 1-56922-039-5

Printed in the United States of America

Produced by John L. Haag

Exclusive Selling Agent:
CREATIVE CONCEPTS PUBLISHING CORP.
410 Bryant Circle, Box 848, Ojai, California 93024

CONTENTS

CONTENTS

The Folk Song Syndrome

By Arnold Shaw

Since the end of World War I, there have been three major folk song revivals in this country. The last spanned the years roughly from 1958 to 1964. The advent of Beatlemania established Rock as the pop music of today. But in its early stage, Rock, or rather rock 'n' roll, was itself a fusion of two 'folk' developments – white country (hillbilly) music and black rhythm-and-blues. And so we may think of today's pop music as folk-oriented.

This fact is suggested by the chart popularity of such folk artists as Judy Collins and Trini Lopez among others. It is given emphasis by the form of today's mainstream music. Gone is the 32-bar song dominated American Pop for over half a century. Today's songs are cast in shapes deriving from 12-bar blues, 16-bar gospel and the verse-chorus forms of folksong. Nor should we disregard the continuing dominance of the instrument that replaced the piano for accompaniment. Today, the guitar, acoustic or electric, Fender or rhythm, is still king.

The traditional definition of folk song stresses two considerations: unknown origin and oral transmission. A third concept is implicit: that the content or experience sung about is indigenous to the singer's background. Purists thus arrange folk singers in a descending order of importance, depending on whether they are **ethnic** in the indigenous sense, **authentic** in that they perform traditional material in a traditional style, or just **popularizers.**

The greatest controversy among folklorists rages around the category of folksingers whose primary concern is to entertain – the bulk of the artists who have recorded material in this collection. The spellbinders of folk music, the **popularizers,** our third category, help attract and build audiences for the ethnics and the authentics. But the purist is less concerned over the diffusion than the dilution of material. Nor is his criticism of the slick and sometimes 'hoked-up' style of the popularizers eliminated by their vital role in triggering revivals.

The group that set off the most recent folk revival with their hit rendition in 1958 of "Tom Dooley" was the Kingston Trio, sometimes called the Brooks Brothers of folk music, because of their high gloss style and the secondary sources of their material. Admitting that they cull tunes from old records and songbooks, the Trio argues: "After all, what is ethnic? It's what's true in the time and place it's sung. Why should we imitate Leadbelly's inflections when we have so little in common with his background and experience?"

Peter, Paul and Mary, who became towering figures of the most recent revival and who popularized the work of folk-poet Bob Dylan, are also sensitive to purist criticism. Peter, Paul and Mary follow a course suggested by Ed McCurdy, a folk performer whose repertoire runs from romper-room to ribald ditties. Rejecting the idea that folk singers music come out of the hills and learn songs at Grandma's crotchety knee, McCurdy proposes that today's folksters call themselves "city-type" singers. Peter, Paul and Mary choose the designation "urban folk singers" and explain: "We try to make the music significant for today."

Joan Baez, another pivotal figure of the '60's folk revival and still a strong voice of today, refuses to take a defensive position. "I don't care very much about where a song came from or why," she has said. "All I care about is how it sounds and the feeling of it." And she adds without being apologetic: "I'm not a pure folk singer. I couldn't be. But I try to be an honest one."

The folk revival of the early '40's was closer in spirit to that of the '60's than of the '20's. Rediscovery of the past was embedded in criticism of the present; if it was nostalgic, it nevertheless looked to the future. And it, too, was infused with the image of the Common Man, then raised by the New Deal and the huge growth of the labor movement. This was the era of Josh White, a favorite of FDR – he became known as the Presidential Minstrel – and the first entertainer to treat folk tunes as art songs on a nightclub floor. Although White learned much of his repertoire by serving as lead-boy for a number of blind bluesmen, including Blind Lemon, he achieved his greatest reknown as a performer in swank Manhattan clubs where his good looks and suave showmanship made him a pre-Belafonte black sex idol. Onstage he made a beguiling figure in an open-necked sports shirt, a lit cigarette stuck behind one ear. To folk singing, if not the blues, he contributed matinee sexuality, bell-like diction and pop appeal, qualities that hardly endeared him to folk purists.

Huddie Ledbetter, son of an ex-slave, became known as Leadbelly because he had "guts of steel and could outwork, outsing and outlast" every other prisoner on chain gangs to which he had been sentenced for murder and attempted homicide. Pardoned by the Governor of Texas when he heard his "Plea For Mercy" during a prison visit, Leadbelly went on to bill himself "King of the Twelve String Guitar." As protege of curator John A. Lomax, he enriched the folk archives of the Library of Congress with recordings of several hundred folk songs, including the chugging "Rock Island Line" and "Midnight Special", a great prison blues song. In the '40's when Leadbelly lived in Manhattan, he played host to the prolific songwriter whose songs include "This Land Is Your Land", regarded as the folk singer's anthem, and "So Long, It's Been Good To Know You", anthem of the dis-possessed dust-bowl farmer. In a mood of depression, Woody Guthrie came to draw strength from Leadbelly, as almost twenty years later young Bob Dylan journeyed to New York to visit Guthrie, his idol.

The supremely-gifted Guthrie wrote many enchanting children's tunes, like the wonderful "Little Sacka Sugar." But he is remembered for the type of topical, New Deal song to be found in "Talking Union", an album he recorded with The Almanacs. In 1949 the Almanacs, sans Guthrie, became the Weavers, a vocal group that rose meteorically with a series of Leadbelly ("Good Night Irene") and Guthrie hits – also "Tzena, Tzena" and "On Top Of Old Smokey" only to fall victim three years later to the McCarthy blacklist. In a dedication written from a hospital bed where he lay incurably ill, Guthrie described his goal: "I am out to sing songs that will prove to you that this is your world and that. . . no matter how hard it's run you down and rolled over you, no matter what color, what size you are, how you are built, I am out to sing songs that make you take pride in yourself and your work."

The most recent revival began in '58 when a group of ex-collegians recorded the ditty of a Civil War veteran hanged for the murder of an inconstant sweetheart. As sung by The Kingston Trio, "Tom Dooley" sold over two million records, propelled the group to stardom, and ignited the generation that had grown up on rock 'n' roll and was then in college. In actuality, rock 'n' roll prepared the ground for the folk craze. Lacking the poetry and beauty of folk song, it nevertheless embodied the ebullient rhythms, the simple, angular harmonies and the stark, primitive melodies. Moreover, rock 'n' roll permitted teenagers to discharge their feelings of conflict with the older generation and led them to seek new values through folk music.

The scope of the '60's revival was broad indeed. It ran the gamut from French love ballads to Irish rebel songs, from country blues to Bluegrass to Israeli horas, from Appalachian mountain tunes to topical songs of protest. What was most significant, however, was not the magnitude of the renaissance but its depth – for it signalized an unmistakable shift in the outlook of young people.

Symbol of this shift and spokesman for its troubled outlook was a 23-year old singer-instrumentalist, "a cross between a beatnik and a choir boy", out of Duluth, Minnesota. Bob Dylan seemed to voice all the generation's complaints against the past and present. As VARIETY observed unsympathetically, these complaints were "against warmongers, Nazis, poverty, injustice, commercial hootenannies, blacklisting, prizefighting, atom fallout, hard-hearted sweethearts, Fabian and the selling and buying of soap. Nowhere was there one word of hope or remedy."

The comment was not entirely accurate. While Dylan had no remedies to propose, it was the hope embodied in "Blowin' In The Wind" that made the song the anthem of the civil rights movement. If the Newport Folk Festival of 1963 had a theme, it was one of racial equality. The appearance of the Freedom Singers, each of whose members had been jailed for civil rights activities, stirred feelings that went beyond the musical import of their singing. Emotions ran higher for Dylan's on-stage stint. And in the closing minutes of the Festival when singers locked hands and sang "We Shall Overcome", there were shouts for Dylan, whose appearance led to an ovation and the singing by performers and audience of "Blowin' In The Wind."

Dylan's was not the only voice of protest on the folk scene of the '60's. Malvina Reynolds of the San Francisco Bay Area dealt with fallout in the delicately ironic ballad "What Have They Done To The Rain." Tom Paxton wrote sardonically of war in "The Willing Recruit," as did Pete Seeger in "Where Have All The Flowers Gone."

The fascination of today's moviegoers and TV-viewers with outlaws, gunfighters, gamblers and convicts is revealed to us by the appeal that made many of them legendary figures as well as the subjects of undying folk ballads.

Perhaps the most interesting of these outlaw songs is the ballad popularized by Leadbelly, a chain gang denizen for many years on murder charges. "Midnight Special" was based on the superstition that if the headlight of a train shone in a prisoner's cell at midnight, he would eventually be freed. Some scholars believe that the song is based less on superstition than symbolism – the swift motion of the train suggesting a future freedom of movement for the prisoner.

The human need for heroes and the celebration of gigantic deeds is amply evident in the folksongs of America. Some of the heroes are mythical. Some are real. But all are legendary.

Early in the life of the country when the land was barren and food was scarce, many men worked at cultivating the soil. None was apparently as dedicated in the planting of apple trees as "Appleseed John" or "Johnny Appleseed", as he was known in earlier versions, and who is, perhaps, a mythical symbol of the early fruit-growers.

Men also made heroes of the superlative and courageous workers in their trades. Casey Jones, the railroad engineer, by whose run you could tell time even if he had to pull 100 freights, remained at his throttle in the face of an impending collision and perished nobly.

Paul Bunyan was a giant among lumbermen whose feats led to outsized exaggerations in folksong: he scooped out the Grand Canyon by dragging his pick, etc. These hyperbolic claims are retained in the contemporary version by Randy Sparks.

And so, it seems apparent that the field of folk music is alive with many strictures and cults. And, for its preservation, we are forever indebted to the painstaking labors of our heroes and criminals alike who have risen from history's dark past to bring their stories to life in song.

–ARNOLD SHAW

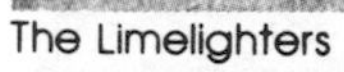

The Limelighters

Laura Nyro

Buffy Sainte-Marie

Gordon Lightfoot

The Byrds

The Kingston Trio

Joan Baez

Joni Mitchell

Simon & Garfunkel

Judy Collins

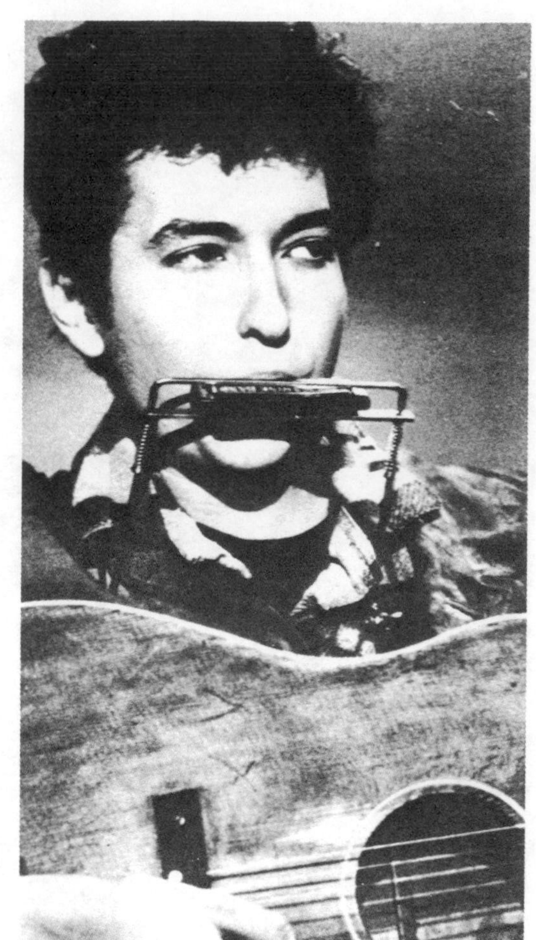
Bob Dylan

The New Christy Minstrels

John Denver

Peter, Paul & Mary

Donovan

Glenn Yarbrough

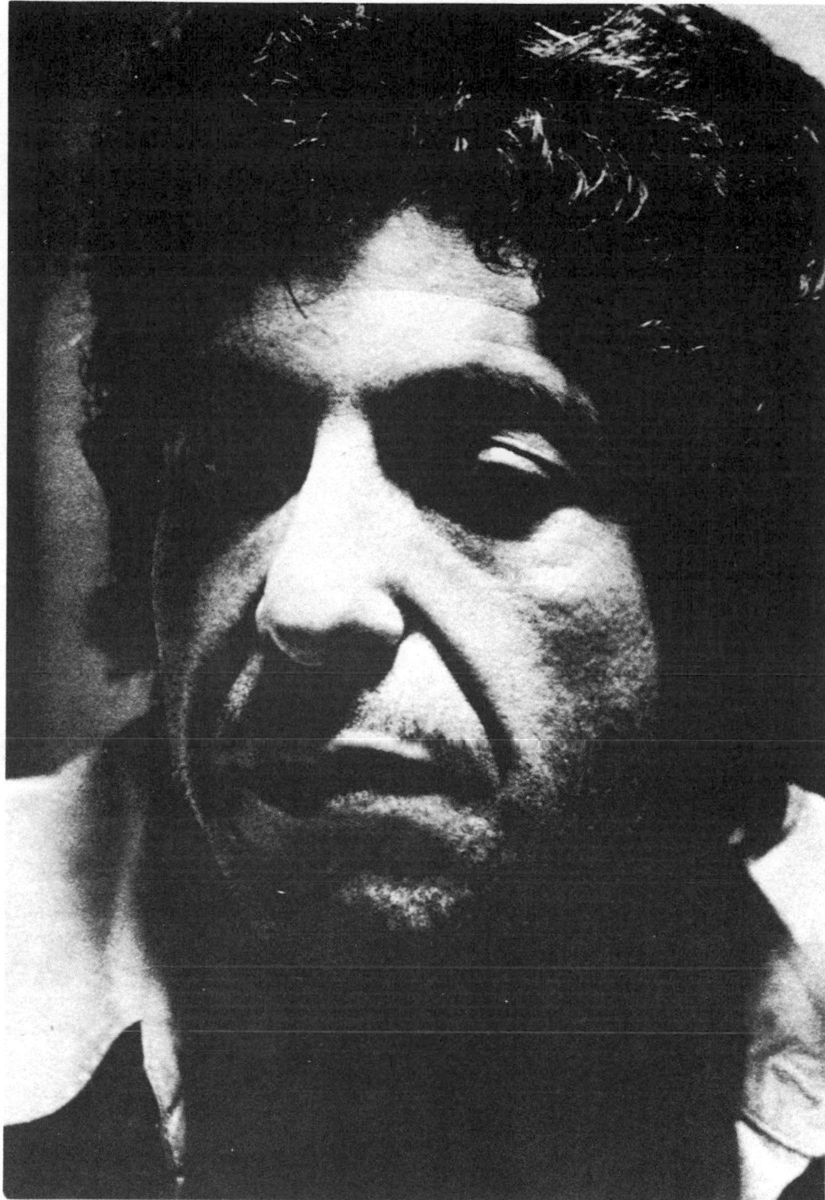
Leonard Cohen

The Brothers Four

AN AMERICAN FOLK TRILOGY

DIXIE / BATTLE HYMN OF THE REPUBLIC / ALL MY TRIALS

Traditional

B♭
E♭ (B♭ bass)
E♭
C7
F7
F7(sus4)
Oh, I wish I was in Dix - ie, a - way, a - way; In Dix - ie - land I'll take my stand, to live and die in Dix - ie, 'cause
mf
Glo - ry, Glo - ry, Hal - le - lu -

Bb7
Eb
-jah!
Glo - ry, Glo - ry, Hal - le -
Bb
D7
-lu - jah!
Glo - ry, Glo - ry, Hal - le -
f
Gm
Gm(F bass)
Eb
Cm7
-lu - jah!
His truth is
F7(sus4)
F7
Eb
Bb(D bass)
C7
Bb
march - ing on.
So,
p

Bb
Fm
hush, lit - tle,chil - dren, don't you cry, You
Bb
Gm
Gm (F bass)
Eb
know your dad dy's bound to die.
Bb
Bb (A bass)
Gm
Gm(F bass)
C7 (E bass)
But All My Tri-als, Lord,
Cm7(F bass)
F7
Bb
Eb
Bb
soon, be o - ver.

BROWN EYED GIRL

Words and Music by Van Morrison

Eb Ab Eb Bb7
In the mis - ty morn - ing fog_ with our hearts a - thump-in', and
Ab Bb7 Eb Cm
you, My Brown Eyed Girl,
Ab Bb7 Eb Bb7
You, my Brown Eyed Girl._ Do you re - mem-
Eb Ab
_ ber when we used to sing:_ Sha la_ la la_ la la_ la la_

2. Whatever happened to Tuesday and so slow
Going down the old mine with a transistor radio
Standing in the sunlight laughing
Hiding behind a rainbow's wall
Slipping and a-sliding
All along the water fall
With you, my Brown Eyed Girl
You, my Brown Eyed Girl.
Do you remember when we used to sing:
Sha la la (etc.)

3. So hard to find my way, now that I'm all on my own
I saw you just the other day, my, how you have grown
Cast my memory back there, Lord
Sometime I'm overcome thinking 'bout
Making love in the green grass
Behind the stadium
With you, my Brown Eyed Girl
With you, my Brown Eyed Girl.
Do you remember when we used to sing:
Sha la la (etc.)

FIVE HUNDRED MILES

Words and Music by Hedy West

G
Em
C
Am7
Chorus 1
miles, a hun-dred miles, a hun-dred miles, a hun-dred miles, You can
mf
D7
G
hear the whis-tle blow a hun-dred miles.
2. Lord, I'm
3.(Not a)
Verse 2&3
one, Lord, I'm two, Lord, I'm three, Lord, I'm four, Lord, I'm
shirt on my back, Not a pen-ny to my name, Lord, I
mp
five hun-dred miles a-way from home. A-way from
can't go back home this-a-way. This-a-

G
Em
C
Chorus 2 & 3
home, a - way from home, a - way from home, a - way from
way, this - a - way, this - a - way, this - a -
mf
Am7
D7
home, Lord, I'm five hun - dred miles a - way from
way, Lord, I can't go back home this - a -
1. G
2. G
D.S. al Coda
home. Not a way.
Instrumental solo
D.S. al Coda
Coda
G
C
D7
Cm
G
You can hear the whis - tle blow a hun - dred miles.
ritard.

COOK WITH HONEY

Words and Music by Valerie Carter

CHORUS
Dbmaj7
Ebm7/Ab
in hand.
I al - ways
cook with hon - ey to sweet - en up the night,
we al - ways cook with hon - ey tell me
how's your ap - pe - tite for some sweet love?

Ebm7/Ab
Dbmaj7
Ebm7/Ab
Dbmaj7
Find - in' fa - vor_with your neigh-
Ebm7/Ab
Db
Ebm7/Ab
Db
bor well it can be so fine,___ it's eas-i - er than
simile
Ebm7/Ab
Dbmaj7
Ebm7/Ab
Dbmaj7
pie to be kind. We've been search-ing for so long___
Ebm7/Ab
Dbmaj7
Ebm7/Ab
Dbmaj7
now our house has turned in - to a home.

Ebm7/Ab Dbmaj7 Ebm7/Ab Dbmaj7 Ebm7/Ab
'Cause I al - ways cook with hon - ey to
Dbmaj7 Ebm7/Ab Dbmaj7
sweet - en up the night. We al - ways cook with hon-
Ebm7/Ab Dbmaj7 Ebm7/Ab Dbmaj7
ey tell me how's your ap - pe - tite for some sweet love?
Ebm7/Ab Dbmaj7 Ebm7/Ab Dbmaj7
Well our door is al - ways o -

Ebm7/Ab Dbmaj7 Ebm7/Ab Dbmaj7
pen and there's al - ways room for more cook-in' where there's
Ebm7/Ab Dbmaj7 Ebm7/Ab Dbmaj7
good love is ne-ver an-y chore
Ebm7/Ab Dbmaj7 Ebm7/Ab Dbmaj7
so come and get to know us there'll be a place set just for you.
Ebm7/Ab Dbmaj7 Ebm7/Ab Dbmaj7
Sweet wine be-fore din-ner that is sure - ly bound to soothe

Ebm7/Ab
Dbmaj7
I al - ways cook with hon -
Ebm7/Ab
Dbmaj7
Ebm7/Ab
ey to sweet - en up the night.
We al - ways
Dbmaj7
Ebm7/Ab
Dbmaj7
Ebm7/Ab
cook with hon - ey tell me how's your ap - pe-tite for some sweet
Repeat And Fade
Dbmaj7
Ebm7/Ab
Dbmaj7
Ebm7/Ab
love?
I al - ways

CALL IT STORMY MONDAY

Words and Music by Aron T-Bone Walker

EXTRA LYRICS

2

Yes, the eagle flies on Friday,
And Saturday I go out to play
Eagle flies on Friday,
And Saturday I go out to play.
Sunday I go to church,
Then I kneel down to pray.

3

Lord have mercy,
Lord have mercy on me
Lord have mercy,
My heart's in misery.
Crazy 'bout my baby,
Yes, send her back to me.

EVERYBODY'S TALKIN'

Words and Music by Fred Neil

F
Cm7
F7
Gm7
C7
thru the pour - in' rain Go - in' where the wea-ther suits my
clothes Bank-in' off of the north-east wind Sail - in' on a sum - mer
Bb
breeze Skip-pin' o - ver the o - cean like a stone.
D. S. al Coda
CODA
Repeat & Fade
And I won't let you leave my love be - hind No,
I won't let you leave my love be - hind And,
I won't let you leave my love be - hind

ACE IN THE HOLE

Words and Music by Dennis Adkins

E♭
Edim
B♭/F
G
C7
Life is a gam-ble, a game we all play but you need to save
put it all on the line for just one roll you've got to have an
1.
F
F7
2.
F
B♭
to Coda
some-thing for a rain-y day. You've
Ace In The Hole.
B♭
If you're head-ed down the one-way street and you're
life deals out a surprise

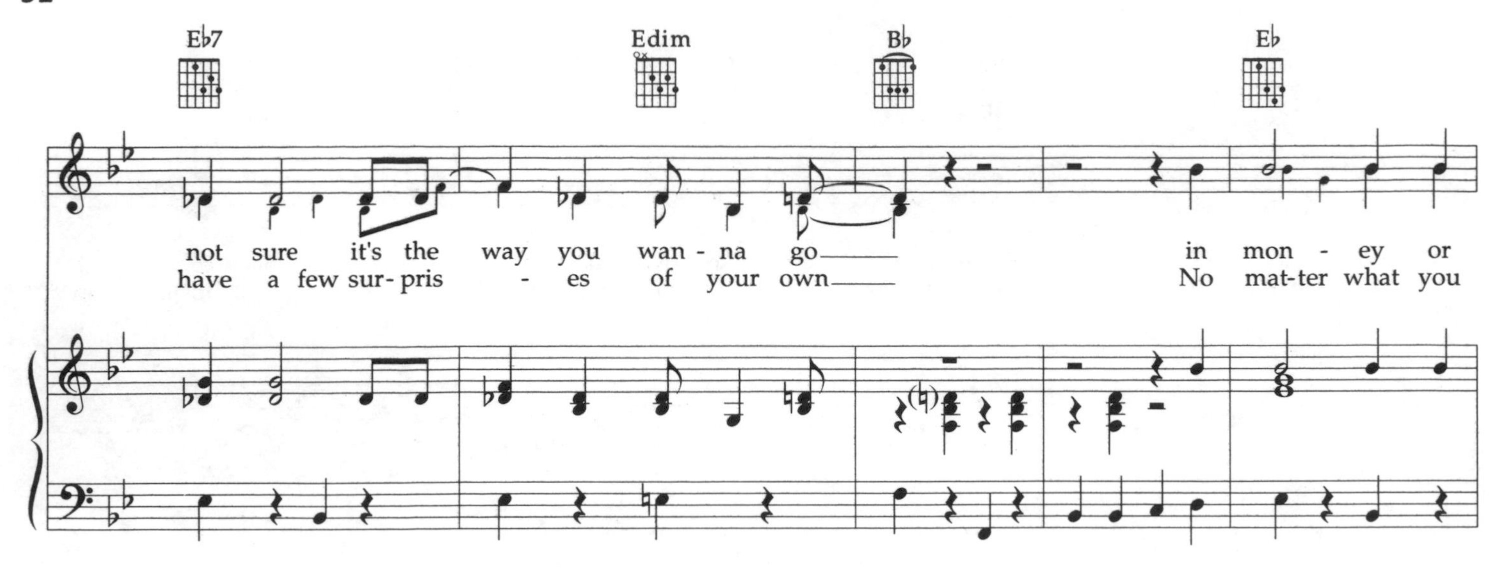
E♭7
Edim
B♭
E♭
not sure it's the way you wan - na go
in mon - ey or
have a few sur - pris - es of your own
No mat - ter what you

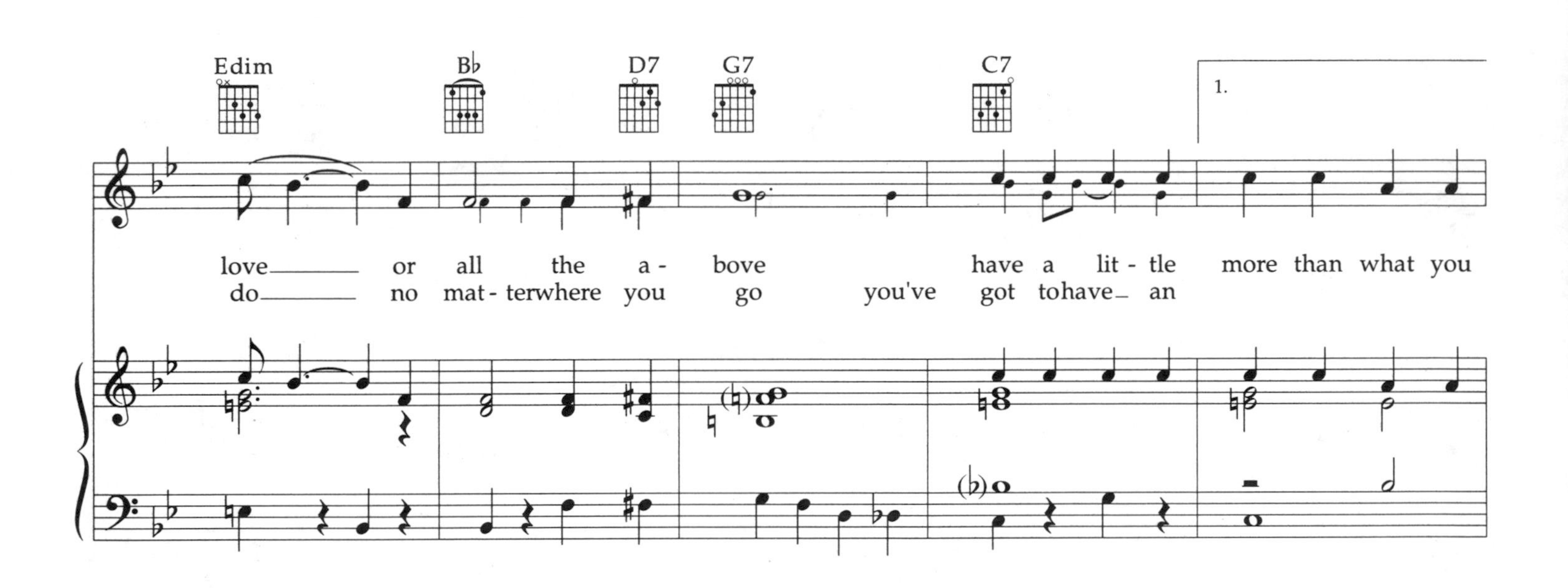
Edim
B♭
D7
G7
C7
1.
love or all the a - bove
have a lit - tle more than what you
do no mat - ter where you go
you've got to have an

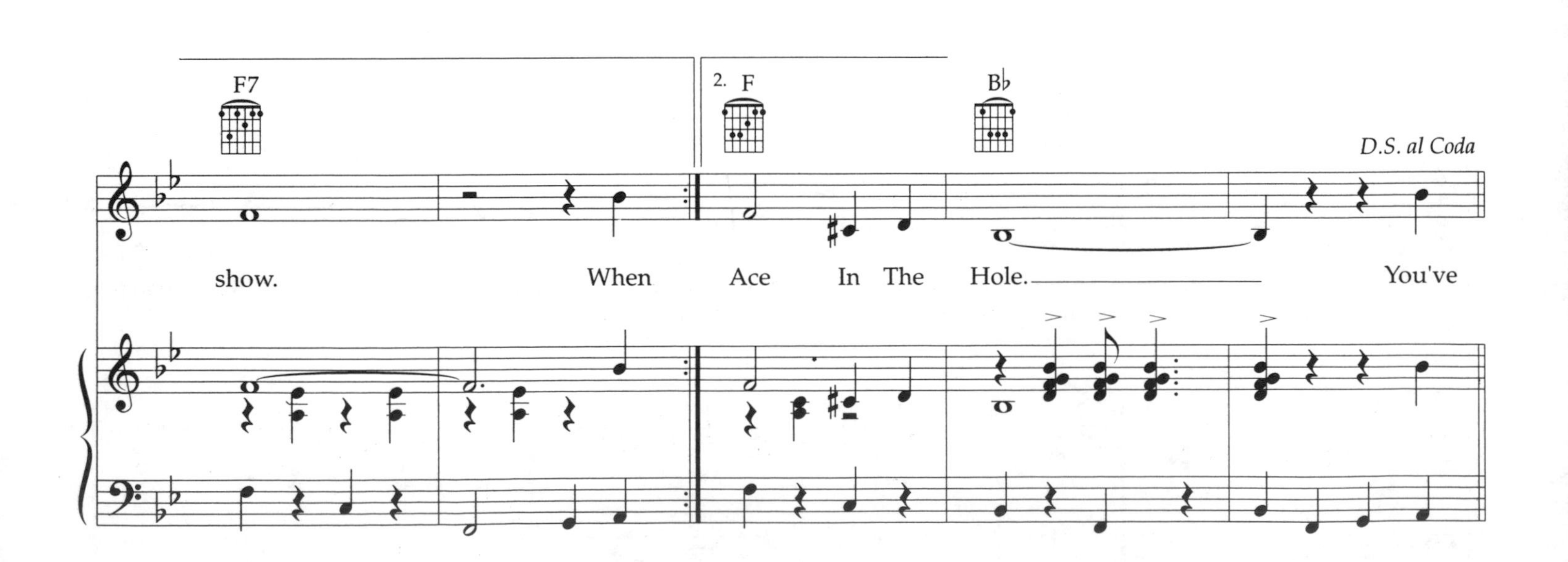
F7
2. F
B♭
D.S. al Coda
show. When
Ace In The Hole.
You've

Coda
B♭
E♭
Edim
B♭
Don't put it all on the line for just one
G
C7
F
B♭
roll you've got to have an Ace In The Hole.
No
E♭
Edim
B♭/F
D7/F♯
G7
C7
mat-ter what you do no mat-ter where you go you've got to have an
F7
B♭
B♭7
E♭
Edim
B♭
F7
B♭
Ace In The Hole.
N.C.

THE FIRST TIME EVER I SAW YOUR FACE

Words and Music by Ewan MacColl

F
G
(sus4)
G7
And the moon and the stars were the
C
to Coda
Bb
gifts you gave To the dark
Bb
C
and the end of the skies.
CODA
C
Bb
And last till the end

2. The first time ever I kissed your mouth
I felt the earth move in my hand,
Like the trembling heart of a captive bird
That was there at my command, my love,
That was there at my command.

3. The first time ever I lay with you
And felt your heart so close to mine,
And I knew our joy would fill the earth
And last till the end of time, my love.
The first time ever I saw your face,
Your face, your face, your face.

I'D LIKE TO TEACH THE WORLD TO SING
(IN PERFECT HARMONY)

Words and Music by B. Backer, B. Davis, R. Cook & R. Greenway

C
Bb
like to hold it in my arms and keep it com - pa - ny.
F
I'd like to see the world for once all
G7
C
stand - ing hand in hand, And hear them ech - o through
Bb
F
Fine
the hills for peace through - out the land.
Fine

F
G7
That's the song I hear, let the world sing to - day.
C
Bb
F
A song of peace that ech-oes on and nev-er goes a-way.
I'd
like to build the world a home and fur-nish it with love,
Grow
ap-ple trees and hon-ey bees and snow white tur-tle doves.
I'd
C7
D. S. al Fine
D. S. al Fine

THE CAT CAME BACK

Words and Music by Johnny Weber

The man around the corner swore he'd kill the cat on sight,
He loaded up his shotgun with nails and dynamite;
He waited and he waited for the cat to come around,
Ninety-seven pieces of the man is all they found.

He gave it to a little boy with a dollar note,
Told him for to take it up the river in a boat;
They tied a rope around its neck, it must have weighed a pound,
Now they drag the river for a little boy that's drowned.

He gave it to a man going up in a balloon,
He told him for to take it to the man in the moon,
The balloon came down about ninety miles away,
Where he is now, well I dare not say.

He gave it to a man going way out west,
Told him for to take it to the one he loved the best;
First the train hit the curve, then it jumped the rail,
Not a soul was left behind to tell the gruesome tale.

The cat it had some company one night out in the yard,
Someone threw a boot-jack, and they threw it mighty hard,
It caught the cat behind the ear, she thought it rather slight,
When along came a brick-bat and knocked the cat out of sight.

Away across the ocean they did send the cat at last,
Vessel only out a day and making the water fast;
People all began to pray, the boat began to toss,
A great big gust of wind came by and every soul was lost.

On a telegraph wire, sparrows sitting in a bunch,
The cat was feeling hungry, thought she'd like 'em for a lunch;
Climbing softly up the pole, and when she reached the top,
Put her foot upon the electric wire, which tied her in a knot.

DANNY BOY

Words by Fred Weatherly
Music from an old Irish Air

C C7 F C Dm G7
gone, and all the ro - ses fall - ing, ... It's you it's you must go and I must
C G7 Am F G7 C
bide. . . . . But come ye back when sum - mer's in the mea - dow, ... Or when the
Am F Em D7 – G7 C F
val - ley's hush'd and white with snow, ... It's I'll be there in sun - shine or in
C Am C F G7 C
sha - dow, . . . Oh, Dan - ny Boy, oh, Dan - ny Boy, I love you so ! . . . .

G7 C C7
p
But when ye come, and all the flow'r's are
cresc.
dolce
sempre legato
F C Em
dy - ing, ... If I am dead, as dead I well may
espress.
F G7 C C7
be, ... Ye'll come and find the place where I am
F C Dm G7 C G7
ly - ing, ... And kneel and say an A - ve there for me ; . . . . And I shall
pp

Am F G7 C
hear, though soft you tread a- bove me, ... And all my
Am F Em D7 – G7
grave will warm-er, sweet-er be, ... For you will
C F C Am
bend and tell me that you love me, ... And I shall
sempre pp
poco cresc. e ritard.
C F G7 C
sleep in peace un- til you come to me! ....
piu lento
rall.
ppp
Ped.

GOTTA TRAVEL ON

Words and Music by Paul Clayton

Verse
G
1. Pop - pa writes to John - ny, but John - ny can't come home.
2. High — sher-iff and po - lice rid - ing af - ter me,
3. Want to see .my hon - ey, want to see her bad,
G7
John - ny can't come home, no, John - ny can't come home; Pop-pa writes to
Rid - ing af - ter me, yes, com - ing af - ter me; High sher-iff and
Want to see her bad, oh, want to see her bad; Want to see my
C D D7
John - ny, but John -ny can't come home, 'Cause he's been on this chain gang too
Po - lice rid - ing af - ter me, And I feel like I've GOT-TA TRA - VEL
hon - ey, want to see her bad, She's the best gal this poor boy ev - er
G
To Verse 1st time,
To Chorus 2nd & 3rd times
long. (To 2nd Verse)
ON. (To Chorus)
had. (To Chorus)
CODA
G D D7
ON. GOT - TA TRAV - EL
(repeat and fade)

LA BAMBA

By Jose Cruz

C7 F C7 F C7
re por ti se - re, por ti se - re. Bam - ba, bam - ba,
F C7 F C7 F
Bam - ba, bam - ba, Bam - ba. Yo no soy mar - i - ne - ro,
C7 F C7 F C7
Yo no soy mar - i - ne - ro, Soy cap - i - tan, Soy cap - i - tan, Soy cap - i - tan.
F C7 F C7 F
Bam - ba, bam - ba, Bam - ba, bam - ba, Bam - ba,
C7 F C7 F
bam - ba, Bam - ba. Pa - ra bai - lar La Bam - ba.
1
2
f
8va

GREEN, GREEN

Words and Music by Randy Sparks and Barry McGuire

VERSE
C
Em
F
C
1. Well, I told my ma - ma on the day I was born, "Don - cha
2. No, there ain't no - bod - y in this whole wide world Gon - na
Optional Girls verse 3. Loved that man with all my heart, I
4. I don't care when the sun goes down, Where I
F
G7
C
Em
cry when you see I'm gone. You know there ain't no wo - man gon - na
tell me how to spend my time. I'm just a good lov - in'
will till the day I die. I was just a stop a -
lay my wea - ry head; Green, green val - ley or a
F
C
F
G7
C
1.
set - tle me down, I just got - ta be trav - el - in' on." A - sing - in'
ram - ble - in' man. Say Bud - dy, could you spare me a dime?
long his way; Nev - er e - ven said good - bye.
rock - y road; It's there I'm gon - na make my bed.

C
2.
3.
4.
Hear me cry-in', it's a
C
F
CHORUS
p-f
Green, Green, it's green, they say, on the far side of the hill;
G7
C7
Green, Green, I'm go-in' a-way To where the
1.
2.
Repeat as needed for Fade out
grass is green-er still.
Spoken:
"Everybody, I want to hear it now!"
grass is green-er still.
To where the

BREAK IT TO ME GENTLY

Words and Music by Diane Lampert and Joe Seneca

C
Cm
G
Bm7
E7
(Tacet)
gent - ly
So my
tears
won't fall to
fast.
If you must
A7
Am7
D7♭9
go
then
go
slow - ly.
Let me
love you
till the
G
G7
C
Bm
last.
The love we shared
for, oh, so long
Am
D7
D7+
G
G7
C
Is such a big part of
me.
If you must take

Bm
A7
D7
your love a - way Take it grad - u - al - ly.
G
G+
C
Cm
G
Bm7
Break it to me gent - ly; Give me time to ease the
E7
(Tacet)
A7
pain. Love me just a lit - tle long - er, 'Cause I'll
Am7
D7♭9
1. G
E♭7
D7
2. G
nev - er love a - gain. gain.
rit.
rall.

THE HOUSE OF THE RISING SUN

Adapted by Art Summit

A7
Dm
me, oh, God, am one. 2. My
when he's on a drunk. 4. Go
Dm
A7
Dm
Moth - er she's a tail - or, She sews those
tell my ba by sis - ter Not to do what
C7
F
A7
Dm
Dm7
new blue jeans. My Fath - er he's a
I have done; To shun that house in
A7
Dm
A7
Dm
gamb - ling man Down in New Or - leans.
New Or - leans They call the Ris - ing Sun.

I'D REALLY LOVE TO SEE YOU TONIGHT

Words and Music by Parker McGee

Dm7
Bb
(C Bass)
C
I called, I guess I real - ly just want - ed to talk to you.
Gm7
C7
Fmaj7
And I was think - in' may - be lat - er on
We could go walk - in' through a wind - y park,
Gm7
C7
Fmaj7
Am7
we could get to - geth - er for a - while. It's been such a long
take a drive a - long the beach or stay at home and watch

Dm7
Bb
(C Bass)
C
time and I real - ly do miss your smile.
T. V. you see it real - ly does - n't mat - ter much to
Bbmaj7
C
(Bb Bass)
Am7
me.
I'm not talk - in' 'bout mov - in' in, and I don't
Bbmaj7
C
(Bb Bass)
Am7
Dm7
wan - na change your life, but there's a
Bbmaj7
C
(Bb Bass)
Am7
Dm7
Bb
(C Bass)
warm wind blow - in' the stars a - round, and I'd real - ly love to see you to - night.

1.
F
2.
F
Dm
Am7
I won't ask for prom - is - es,
Bbmaj7
C
F
Dm
so you don't have to lie.
We've both played that
Am7
Bb
(C Bass)
C
D.S. and fade
game be - fore;
say I love you, then say good - bye.

(At The) END OF A RAINBOW

Lyric by Sid Jacobson   Music by Jimmy Krondes

G7 (opt.) C Em Dm7 G7
flow, At THE END of a high-way, There's no place you can go; But just
C Am7 1. Dm7 G7 C G#dim Am
tell me you love me And you are on-ly mine, And our love will go
Am7 Dm7 G7 C (opt.) 2. Dm7 G7 Dm7 G7
on Till THE END of time. At THE you are on-ly mine, And our
8va
mf
C Am Dm G9 G7 C
love will go on Till THE END of time.
Am7 Dm7 G7 C
Till THE END of time.
rall.

JUST A LITTLE BIT OF RAIN

Words and Music by Fred Neil

B♭
E♭
F7
B♭
E♭
F7
sad __ times
And just A LIT - TLE BIT OF
RAIN.
And just A LIT - TLE BIT OF
B♭
B♭
E♭
RAIN. ______
And if I look back, ___
I'll re - mem - ber all the
B♭
E♭
B♭
E♭
F7
good times
Warm ___ days filled with sun - shine,
And just A LIT - TLE BIT OF
B♭
E♭
F7
B♭
RAIN.
And just A LIT - TLE BIT OF
RAIN. ______
Rit.

LEMON TREE

Words and Music by Will Holt

E♭
B♭7
Tree ver - y pret-ty, And the lem-on flow-er is sweet, But the fruit of the poor
E♭
lem-on is a thing one can-not eat. Lem - on Tree ver - y pret-ty, And the
B♭7
lem-on flow-er is sweet, But the fruit of the poor lem-on is a thing one can-not
E♭
F
E♭
1.2.
3.
eat.
2. Be-
3. One
eat.

MICHAEL

Adapted by Rev. Earl Osborn

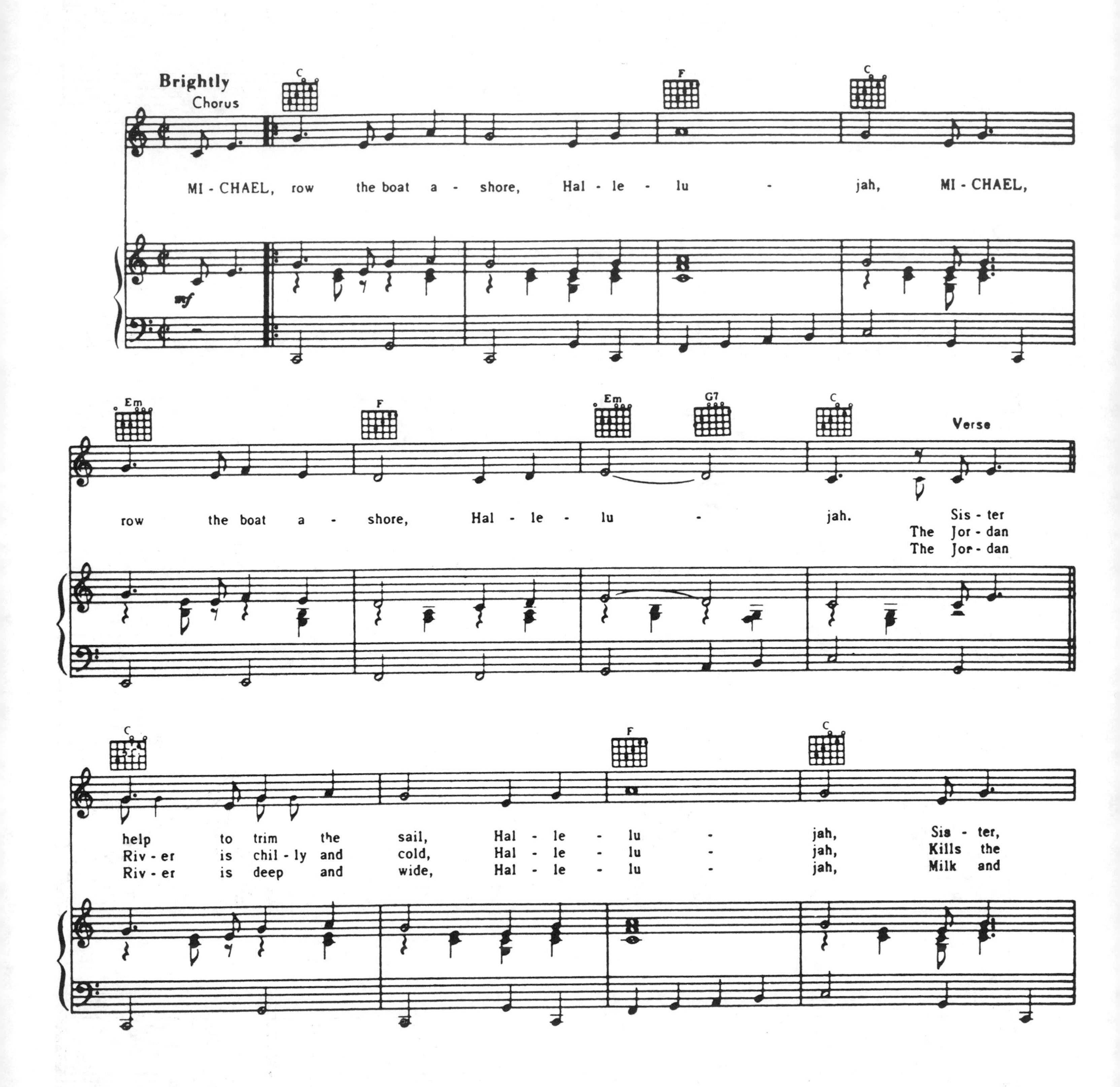

Em
F
Em
G7
1-2 C
3 C
help to trim the sail, Hal - le - lu - jah. MI - CHAEL
bod - y but not the soul, Hal - le - lu - jah. MI - CHAEL
hon - ey on the oth - er side, Hal - le - lu - jah. MI - CHAEL
Chorus
C
F
C
Row the boat a - shore, Hal - le - lu - jah, MI - CHAEL,
Em
F
Em
G7
C
Row the boat a - shore, Hal - le - lu - jah.
rall.

I CAN SEE CLEARLY NOW

Words and Music by Johnny Nash

G
D
To Coda
1
C
bright – sun shin-y day,
It's gon-na be a bright,
G
D
2
bright — sun shin - y day.
F
C
Look all a - round — there's noth-ing but blue sky,
cresc.
F
A
G
F
A
Look straight a-head — noth - ing but blue sky.

D♭m
G
D♭m
G
C
D6
A
poco dim.
D. S. al Coda
D
CODA
C
G
It's gon-na be a bright, bright — sun shin- y day.-
1 D
2 D

SCARBOROUGH FAIR

Adaptation by Woody Hayes

Slowly, with feeling

Dm Dm7 Gm Am Em Cmaj7

Are you go - ing to Scar - bor - ough
Tell her to make me a cam - bric

Dm Am Am7 Dm Am7

Fair? Pars - ley, sage, ____ rose -
shirt, Pars - ley, sage, ____ rose -

Dm G Am Dm Am Dm Bb

ma - ry and thyme; Re - mem - ber
ma - ry and thyme; With - out any

F C F Am7 Gm
me to one that lives there, For
seam or fine nee - dle work, And
Dm G C Gm C Dm
once she was a true love of mine.
then she'll be a true love of mine.
Dm Gm Am C Dm B♭
Oh, will you find me an a - cre of land,
Oh, will you reap it with a sick - le of leath - er,

Am F B♭ F Am G Em7 A F7
Pars - ley, sage, rose - ma - ry and thyme; be -
Pars - ley, sage, rose - ma - ry and thyme; and
B♭ F C F Am7
tween the sea foam and the sea sand Or
tie it all up with a pea - cock's feath - er, Or
Gm F Em Dm Am B♭ C Dm D
nev - er be a true love of mine.
nev - er be a true love of mine.
rit.

HERE COMES THE SUN

Words and Music by George Harrison

A
D
E7
Lit-tle dar-ling, It feels like years since it's been here.
Lit-tle dar-ling, It seems like years since it's been here.
Lit-tle dar-ling, It seems like years since it's been clear.
A
Dmaj7
B7
Here Comes The Sun, Here Comes The Sun, (and I say,)
A
D
A
Bm7
A
E7
A
E7
To Coda
"It's all- right."
E7
C
G
D
A
E7

C
G
D
1.2.3.4.
A
E7
Sun, sun, sun, Here it comes.
5.
A
E7
A
E7
D. S. al ⊕ Coda
comes.
⊕ Coda
A
Dmaj7
B7
A
Here Comes_The Sun,
Here Comes_The Sun,
It's all - right.
D
A
Bm7
A
E7
1.
A
2.
C
G
D
A
It's all - right.

UNTIL IT'S TIME FOR YOU TO GO

Words and Music by Buffy Sainte-Marie

E7
F7
Am7
Bbm7
D7
Eb7
1.
G
Ab
and here we'll stay un - til it's time for you to go.
and here you'll stay un - til it's time for you to
D
Eb
2.
G
Ab
Ab
A
4 fr.
Yes, we're go.
F7
F#7
G
Ab
3 fr.
Ab
A
4 fr.
F7
F#7
Don't ask why,
don't ask
G
Ab
3 fr.
B7
C7
Em sus4
Fm sus4
how,
don't ask for - ev - er,
cresc.
mf

Em
Em sus4
A7
D
Fm
Fm sus4
B♭7
E♭
love me
now.
This love of
dim.
mp
mf
G
G/F♯
Bm7-5/F
E7
A♭
A♭/G
Cm7-5/G♭
F7
mine had no be-gin-ning, it has no end,
I was an
Am
Am(maj7)
Am7
D7
B♭m
B♭m(maj7)
B♭m7
E♭7
oak, now I'm a wil-low; now I can bend.
And though I'll
G
G/F♯
Bm7-5/F
E7
A♭
A♭/G
Cm7-5/G♭
F7
nev-er in my life see you a-gain,
still I'll

Am7
D7
G
Ab
Bbm7
Eb7
Ab
A
stay un-til it's time for you to go.
F7
G
Ab
F7
F#7
Ab
A
F#7
Don't ask why of me, don't ask
G
B7
Em
Ab
C7
Fm
how of me, don't ask for - ev - er of
cresc. poco a poco
Am7
A7
D
Bbm7
Bb7
Eb
me, love me, love me now. You're not a
f

G G/F♯ Bm7-5/F E7 Am
A♭ A♭/G Cm7-5/G♭ F7 B♭m
dream, you're not an an-gel, you're a man, I'm not a queen, I'm a
dim. poco a poco
Am(maj7) Am7 D7 G G/F♯
B♭m(maj7) B♭m7 E♭7 A♭ A♭/G
wom-an, take my hand. We'll make a space in the lives that we'd
mf
Bm7-5/F E7 Am7 D7
Cm7-5/G♭ F7 B♭m7 E♭7
planned, and here we'll stay un-til it's time for you to
molto rit.
G A♭ F G
A♭ A F♯ A♭
4 fr.
go.
a tempo
Ped.

SATURDAY NIGHT

Words and Music by Randy Sparks

F
C G7 C G7
Cry on yer pil-low when things go wrong, And wait for Sat-ur-day Night. Let me tell you 'bout
go-in' to the dogs, you can see it more and more,
We're sort-a qui-et and kind-a home - spun, But we're
C G7 C G7
C G7 G7
C
Spec-'lly on a Sat-ur-day Night.
wild on a Sat-ur-day Night! Ea-sy now!
CHORUS
C F C Am G7
mp
Sat-ur-day Night, Sat-ur-day Night, We all get to-geth-er on Sat-ur-day Night.
C C7 F Fm
cresc.
We'll do things you've nev-er seen. Ain't com-in' home 'til twelve fif-teen! On a
f
C C7 F C G7 C G7
Repeat as needed for Fade-out
Sun-day or a Mon-day you can't do it right. Ain-cha glad we got Sat-ur-day Night? Ain-cha

SLOOP JOHN B.

Words and Music by Johnny Weber

Bbm F C7 F
I feel so break up, I want to go home.
I feel so break up, I want to go home.
This is the worst trip since I been born.
Chorus
F Bb F Bb F
So hoist up The John B. Sails, See how the main - sail sets.
Bb F C7
Send for the Cap - tain a - shore, let me go home. Let me go
F F7 Bb Bbm F
home, Let me go home, 1.2. I feel so break up
3. This is the worst trip
C7 F F
I wan - na go home. 2. The
since I been 3. The born.
1-2
3
mp

HEY LOLLY, LOLLY

Words and Music by Johnny Weber

Married men will keep your secret,
Hey lolly, lolly lo.
Single boys will talk about you,
Hey lolly, lolly lo.

Two old maids a-sittin' in the sand. . .
Each one wishin' that the other was a man. . .

I have a girl, she's ten feet tall. . .
Sleeps in the kitchen with her feet in the hall. . .

Everybody sing the chorus. . .
Either you're against us or you're for us. . .

The purpose of this little song. . .
Is to make up verses as you go along. . .

(There Was A) TALL OAK TREE

Words and Music by Dorsey Burnette

C G Em A7
sky a - bove The cre - a - tor looked down and saw
out of the ground He tempt - ed wo - man and that
D7 Am7 D7 1. G C G
ev - 'ry - thing was love, love, love. Then - a
spread sin all a -
2. G C G G7 C G
round, all a - round, all a - round. If she'd - a left that ap - ple on the
D7 G G7 C G
ap - ple tree There'd be no tears and sor - row, we'd live e -
D7 Am7 G D7 C G
ter - nal - ly. But a - long came man to burn the

C G C G
oak tree down___ And now the bab-bl-in' brook___ is a
C G C G
sol-id ground. Now the moun-tain high don't
C G Em A7 D7 G D7
stand so high_ And there's a cloud of smoke that cov-ers up the clear blue sky_
G C G
There was a TALL OAK TREE_ There was a
C G C G
TALL OAK TREE_ There was a TALL OAK TREE.___
rit

MIDNIGHT SPECIAL

Adapted by Sammy Cash

2. Well if you're ever in Houston,
   You'd better walk on by
   Oh, you'd better not gamble, boy
   I say you'd better not fight.
   Well now, the sheriff, he'll grab you
   And his boys will pull you down
   And then before you know it
   You're penitentiary-bound.
   (To Chorus) A-let the Midnight Special etc.

3. Here comes Miss Lucy
   How in the world do you know?
   I know by her apron
   And by the dress she wore.
   An umbrella on her shoulder
   A piece of paper in her hand
   She gonna see the sheriff
   To try to free her man.
   (To Chorus) A-let the Midnight Special etc.

SUZANNE

Words and Music by Leonard Cohen

cra - zy and that's why you want to be there; And she
cer - tain on - ly drown - ing men could see Him He
hon - ey on our la - dy of the har - bour; And she
Em
F
feeds you tea and o - ran - ges that came all the way from Chi - na, And
said "All men shall be sail - ors, then, un - til the sea shall free them," But
shows you where to look a - mid the gar - bage and the flow - ers. There are
C
just when you want to tell her that you have no love to give her she
He Him - self was bro - ken long be - fore the sky would o - pen. For -
he - roes in the sea - weed, There are chil - dren in the morn - ing, they are

Dm
gets you on her wave length and lets the riv - er an - swer that you've
sak - en, al - most hu - man, He sank be - neath your wis - dom like a
lean - ing out for love, and they will lean that way for - ev - er while
C
al - ways been her lov - er. And you
stone. And you
Suz - anne holds her mir - ror. And you
Chorus
Em
F
want to trav - el with her, And you want to trav - el blind, And you
want to trav - el with Him, And you want to trav - el blind, And you
want to trav - el with her, And you want to trav - el blind, And you
mf

C
Dm
think you may - be trust her, 'Cause she's touched your per-fect bod-y, with her
think you may - be trust Him, For he's touched your per-fect bod-y, with His
think may-be you'll trust her, For you've touched her per-fect bod-y, with your
1.2.
C
mind.
mind.
2. And
3. Suz -
3.
C
mind.
ritard

SEVENTH SON

Words and Music by Willie Dixon

2nd Verse
Eb Bb7+ Eb Bb7+ Eb Bb7+ Eb Bb7+
I can tell your fu-ture, if we come to pass,— I can do things to you make your heart feel glad;
mp
Eb Bb7+ Eb Bb7+ Eb Bb7+ Eb Eb7
D. S.
Look in the sky, pre-dict the rain,— Tell when a wo-man's got an - oth-er man.— I'm the go
D. S.
3rd Verse
Eb Bb7+ Eb Bb7+ Eb Bb7+ Eb Bb7+
I can talk these words—that will sound so sweet,—They will e-ven make your lit-tle heart skip a beat;
mp
Eb Bb7+ Eb Bb7+ Eb Bb7+ Eb Eb7
D. S. al Fine
Heal the sick, raise the dead,— Make the lit - tle girls— talk out of their heads.—I'm the
D. S. al Fine

AT SEVENTEEN

Words and Music by Janis Ian

C
mar - ried young and then — re - tired. —
on - ly get what they — de - serve." —
choos - ing sides for bas ket - ball. —
The
The
It was

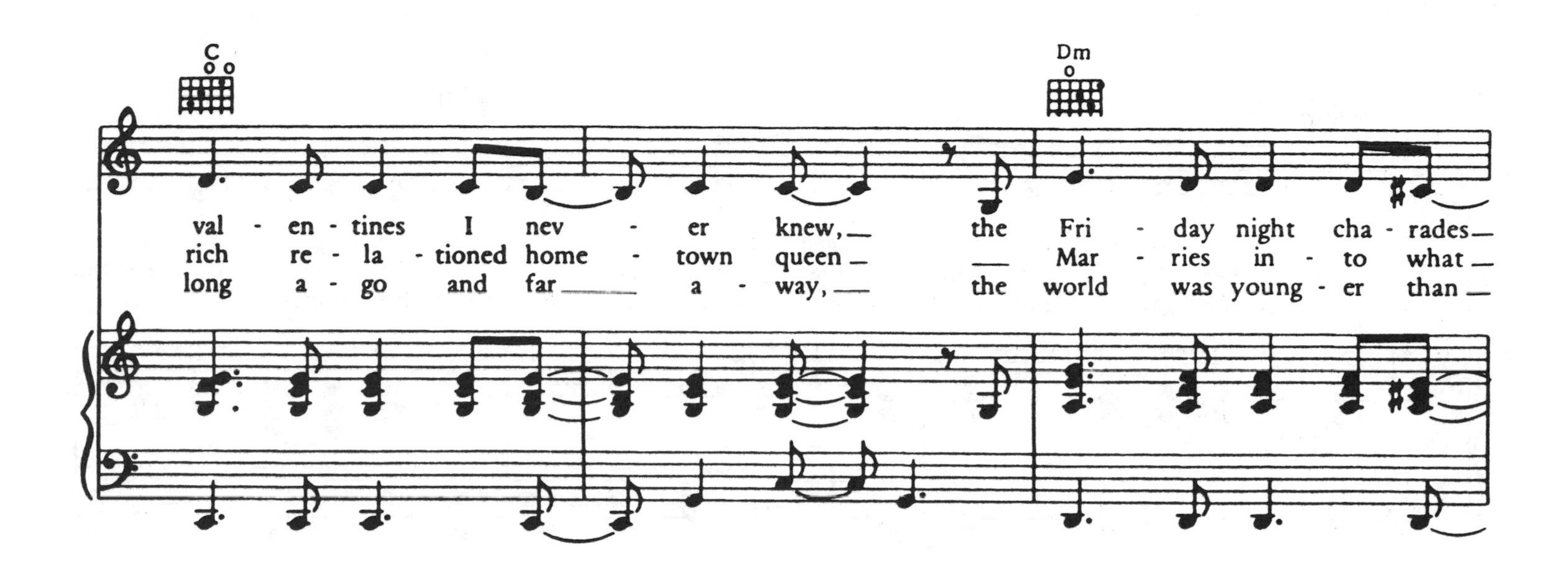
C
Dm
val - en - tines I nev - er knew, — the Fri - day night cha - rades —
rich re - la - tioned home - town queen — — Mar - ries in - to what —
long a - go and far — a - way, — the world was young - er than —

G7
— of youth — Were spent on one — more beau - ti - ful, — At
— she needs: — A guar - an - tee — of com - pa - ny — And
— to - day, — And dreams were all — they gave — for free — to

C
sev - en - teen, I learned the truth. And
ha - ven for the eld - er - ly. Re-
ug - ly duck - ling girls like me. We all

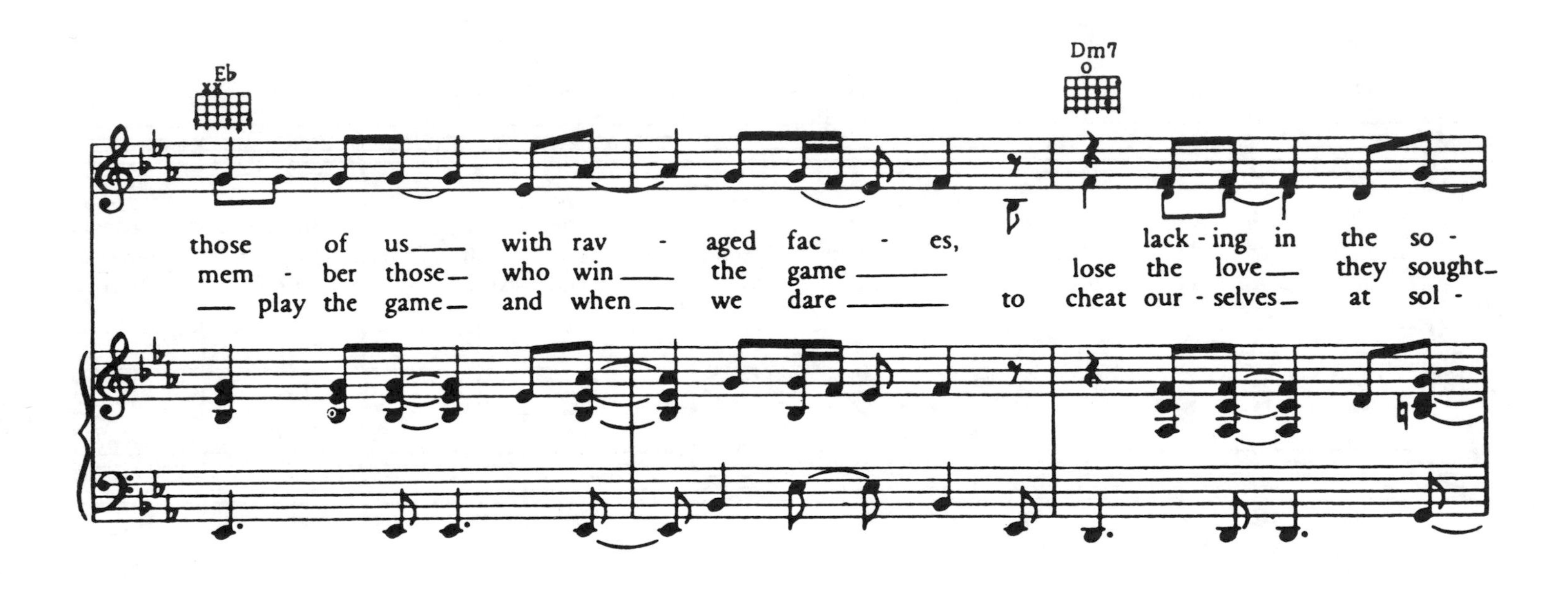
Eb
Dm7
those of us with rav - aged fac - es, lack - ing in the so -
mem - ber those who win the game lose the love they sought
play the game and when we dare to cheat our - selves at sol -

G7
Cm7
3 fr.
Fm7
- cial grac - es, Des - p'rate - ly re - mained at home in -
to gain In de - ben - tures of qual - i - ty and
- i - taire In - vent - ing lov - ers on the phone, re -

Cm7
3 fr.
Fm7
Ab
4 fr.
vent - ing lov - ers on the phone Who called to say, "Come dance
du - bi - ous in - teg - ri - ty. Their small town eyes will gape
pent - ing oth - er lives un - known That call and say, "Come dance
G7
Cm7
3 fr.
Fm7
with me," and mur - mured vague ob - scen - i - ties.
at you in dull sur - prise when pay - ment due
with me," and mur - mur vague ob - scen - i - ties
Dm7
G7
1. 2.
It is - n't all it seems at sev - en - teen. 2. A
Ex - ceeds ac - counts re - ceived at sev - en - teen. 3. To
at ug - ly girls like me at sev - en - teen.
3.
C
Cmaj7

ON AND ON

Words and Music by
Stephen Bishop

C
Am7(add D)
3 fr.
Dm7
F/G
C
A7sus4
A7
love with ol'__ Sam.__ Take__ him from the fire in-to the fry-ing pan.__ On and
stars from the__ sky.__ Puts on Si-na-tra and__ starts to cry.__ On and
dream and stay__ tan.__ Toss up my heart to see where it lands.__ On and
Dm7
F/G
Cmaj7
on, she just keeps__ on try - ing.__ And she smiles__ when she feels__
on, he just keeps__ on try - ing.__ And he smiles__ when he feels__
on, I just keep__ on try - ing.__ And I smile__ when I feel__
A7sus4
A7
Dm7
F/G
__ like cry - ing. On__ and on, on and on, on__ and on.__
__ like cry - ing. On__ and on, on and on, on__ and on.__
__ like dy - ing. On__ and on, on and on, on__ and on.__

C
Am7(add D)
3 fr.
To Coda
1.
2.
When the
Fmaj7
Em7
Dm7
F/G
first time is the last time, it can make you feel so bad.
Cmaj7
But if you know it, show it. Hold
Am7
D9
4 fr.
Fmaj7/G
on tight. Don't let her say good - night.

D. S. al Coda
C
Am7(add D)
3 fr.
Got the
Coda
Dm7
F/G
On and on, on and on, on and on.
A7
On and on, on and on, on and on.
C(add D)
rit.

BALLIN' THE JACK

Words by Jim Burris
Music by Chris Smith

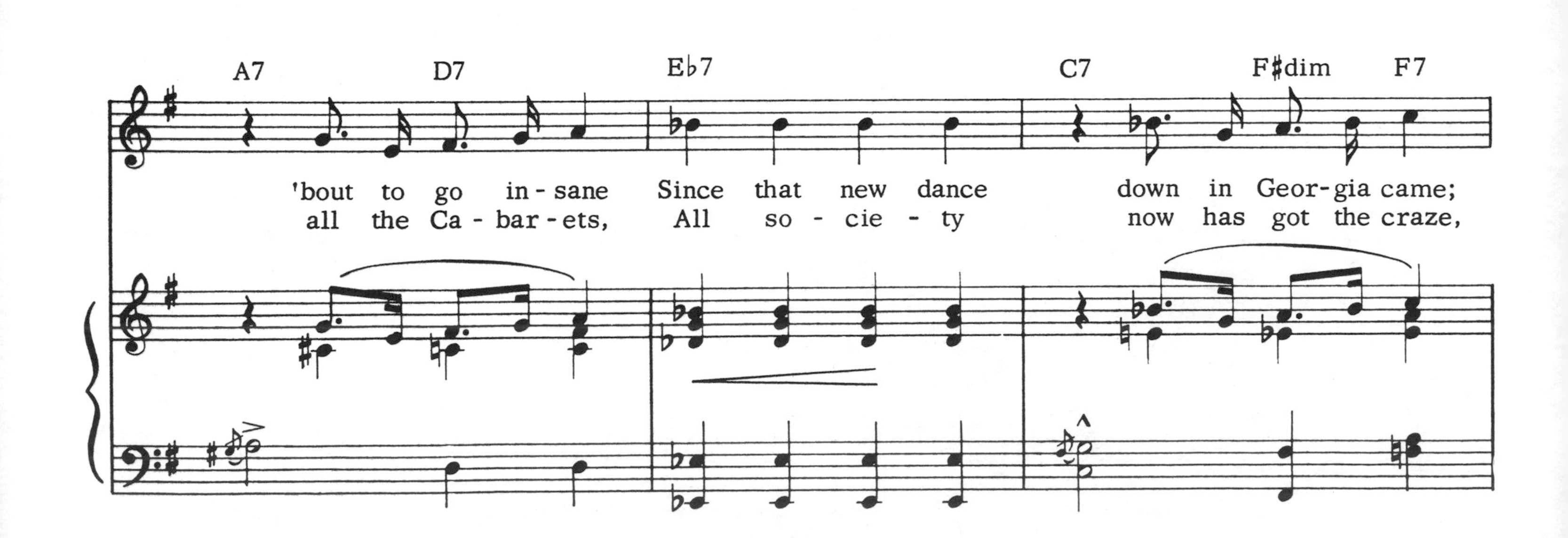

Gb7
Eb7
I'm the on - ly per - son who's to blame, I'm the par - ty in - tro - duced it
It's the best dance done in mo - dern days, That is why I rave a - bout it
D D7 G A7 D7 Eb7
there, so! Give me cre - dit to know a thing or two, Give me cre - dit
so. Play some good Rag that will make you prance; Old folks, young folks,
p
C7 F#dim F7 Gb7
for spring - ing some - thing new; I will show this lit - tle dance to you.
all try to do the dance, Join right in now while you got the chance
Eb7 D F7
When I do you'll say that it's a bear.
Once a - gain the steps to you I'll show.

Chorus (not too fast)
G7
p-f
First you put your two knees close up tight, Then you
C7
sway 'em to the left, then you sway 'em to the right,
F7
Step a-round the floor kind of nice and light, Then you
B♭
D7
twis' a-round and twis' a-round with all your might,
E♭dim
D7

G7
Stretch your lov - in' arms straight out in space, Then you
C7
do the Ea - gle Rock with sty - le and grace, Swing your
G♭7
Bb F♯dim Gm G7 Cm G Cm Cm7(♭5)
foot way 'round then bring it back, Now that's what I call
1. F7 Bb
"Ball - in' the Jack."
2. F7 Bb
"Ball - in' the Jack."
fz

TURN AROUND

Words and Music by Malvina Reynolds,
Allen Greene and Harry Belafonte

Fm7
Bb7
Eb
CHORUS
Eb
Gm
young girl, go-ing out of the door.
young wife, with babes of your own.
Turn A-round, Turn A-round, Turn A-
Ab
Gm
Ab
Eb
Bb7
Eb
1.
round and you're a young girl, go-ing out of the door.
a young wife, with babes of your
Eb
2.
Eb
Gm
own. Turn A-round, Turn A-round, Turn A-
Ab
Gm
Ab
Eb
Bb7
Eb
round and you're a young wife, with babes of your own.
(slowly)

YOU BETTER MOVE ON

Words and Music by Arthur Alexander

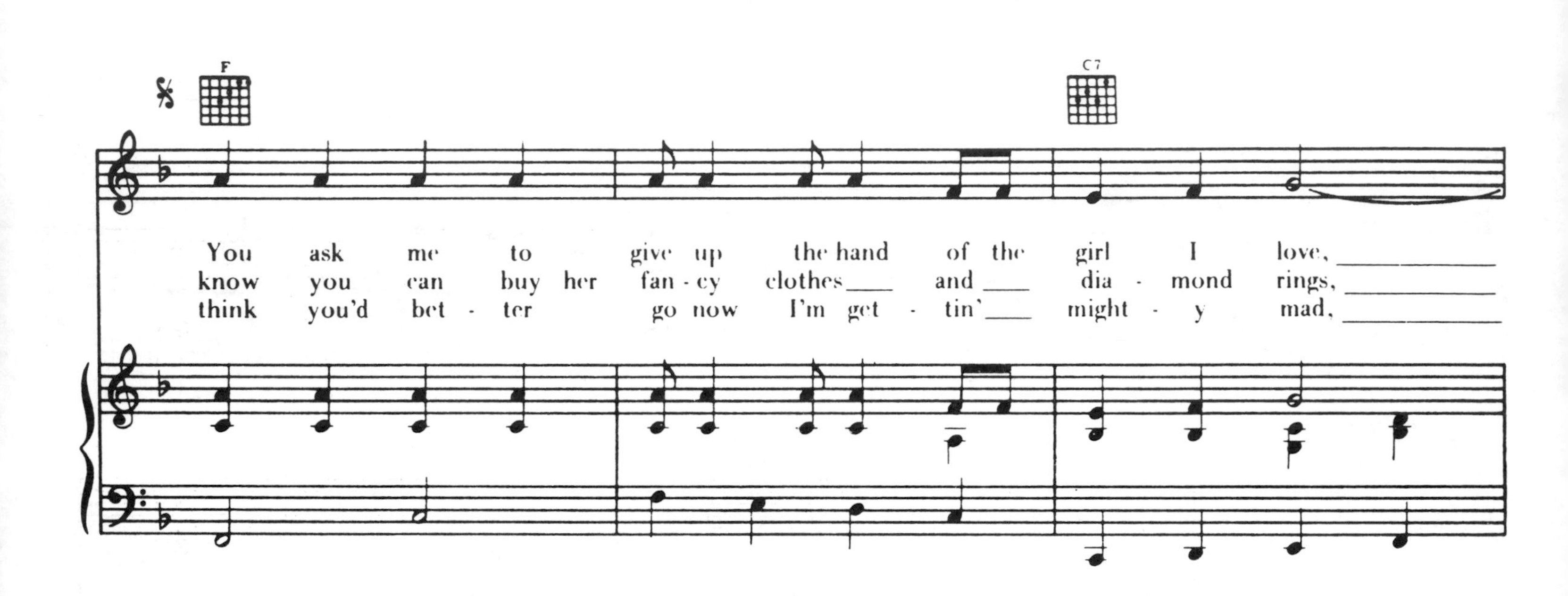

F
F7
worth-y of.
But who are you
out those things.
Still you beg me
ev - er had.
May be I would

Last time To Coda
to tell her who to love?
That's
oh, to set her free,
But my friend that'll
oh, but I love her so,
I'm nev-er gon-na

F
1.
C7
up to her,
yes and the Lord a - bove,

F
C7
You Bet - ter Move On. You Bet - ter Move On. Well, I
2.
F
C7
F
F7
nev - er be, __ You Bet - ter Move On.
B♭
F
F7
I can't blame you for lov - in' her, __
B♭
F
Can't you un - der - stand, ______ man, she's my ___ girl, ___

F7
B♭
yeah. And I, Lord. I, I'm nev-er gon-na
F
G7
let her go; Cuz I, Lord,
C7
D.S. al Coda
I, you know that I love her so. Well, I
Coda
F
C7
F
C7
Repeat and Fade
let her go, You Bet-ter Move On. You Bet-ter Move On. You Bet-ter Move On.

WHERE HAVE ALL THE FLOWERS GONE?

Words and Music by Pete Seeger

C
G7
Where Have All The Flow - ers Gone? The girls have picked them ev - 'ry one.
Where have all the young girls gone? They've tak - en hus - bands ev - 'ry one.
Where have all the young men gone? They're all in u-ni - form.
F
G7
C
F
G7
Oh, when will they ev-er learn? Oh, when will they ev-er
Oh, when will they ev-er learn? Oh, when will they ev-er
Oh, when will they ev-er learn? Oh, when will they ev-er
1. 2.
C
learn?
learn?
3.
C
learn?
rit.
p

4. Where have all the soldiers gone? Long time passing.
   Where have all the soldiers gone? Long time ago.
   Where have all the soldiers gone?
   They've gone to graveyards, every one.
   Oh, when will they ever learn?
   Oh, when will they ever learn?

5. Where have all the graveyards gone? Long time passing.
   Where have all the graveyards gone? Long time ago.
   Where have all the graveyards gone?
   They're covered with flowers, every one.
   Oh, when will they ever learn?
   Oh, when will they ever learn?

6. Where Have All The Flowers Gone? Long time passing.
   Where Have All The Flowers Gone? Long time ago.
   Where Have All The Flowers Gone?
   Young girls picked them, every one.
   Oh, when will they ever learn?
   Oh, when will they ever learn?

PETE SEEGER

A WORRIED MAN

Words and Music by John Reynolds

RED WING

Words by Thurland Chattaway
Music by Kerry Mills

Bb7 Eb Cm F7 Bb7 Eb
brave and gay, he rode one day to bat-tle far a-way.
far, far a-way, her war-ri-or gay, fell brave-ly in the fray.
CHORUS
Ab Eb
Now, the moon shines to-night on pret-ty RED-WING,
mp-f
Bbdim Bb7 Eb
the breeze is sigh-ing, the night bird's cry-ing, For a-
Ab Eb Bbdim Bb7
far 'neath his star her brave is sleep-ing, While Red Wing's weep-ing
1 Eb 2 Eb
her heart a-way. Now, the way.

WE'LL SING IN THE SUNSHINE

Words and Music by Gale Garnett

F
Bb
But though I'll nev - er love you, I'll
But, dar - ling, don't cling to me; I'll
man,) Just take what they may give you And
You'll of - ten speak a - bout me And
C7
Gm7
C9
F
Fmaj7
F7
Bb
Gm7
C7
live with you one year And We'll Sing In The Sun - shine,
soon be out of sight. But we can sing in the sun - shine,
give but what you can. And you can sing in the sun - shine,
this is what you'll say: We sang in the sun - shine,
1,2,3. We'll laugh ev - 'ry
4. We laughed ev - 'ry
mf
F
Fmaj7
F7
Bb
Gm
Gm7
C9
day; We'll Sing In The Sun - shine And I'll be on my
day; We sang in the sun - shine, Then he went on his
(she) (her)
F
1,2,3.
Gm7
C7
4
F
Bb
F
way.
2. I'll
3. My
4. And way.
mp
rit.
f

THERE BUT FOR FORTUNE

Words and Music by Phil Ochs

Am
D7
G
life has gone stale. And I'll show you a
sleeps out in the rain. And I'll show you a
Em
C
Am
young man with so man-y rea - sons why And
young man with so man-y rea - sons why And
Bm
Em
Am
there but for for - tune go you or
there but for for - tune go you or

3. Show me the whiskey that stains on the floor.
Show me the drunkard as he stumbles out the door.
And I'll show you a young man with so many reasons why,
And there but for fortune go you or I. Mm hm.

4. Show me the country where the bombs had to fall,
Show me the ruins of the buildings once so tall.
And I'll show you a young land with so many reasons why,
And there but for fortune go you and I, you and I.